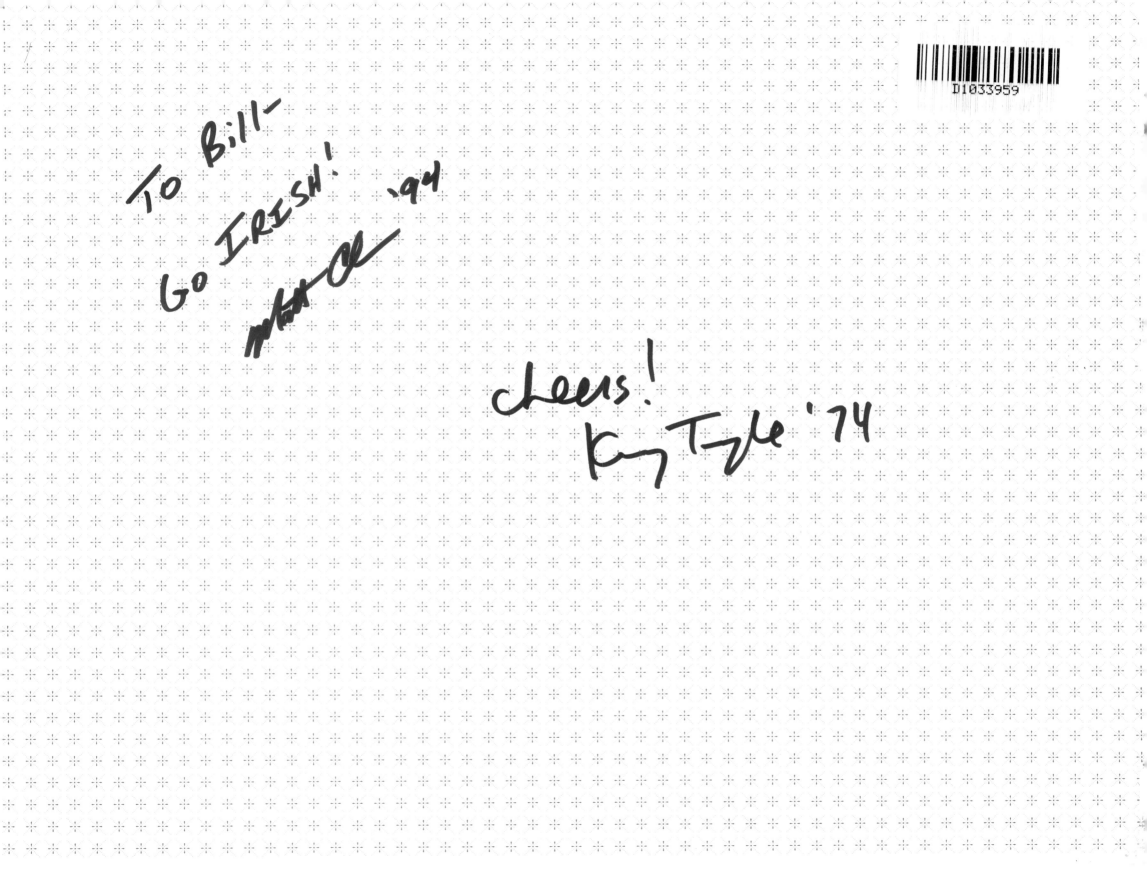

To Bill—
Go IRISH!
'94

cheers!
Kenny Taylor '74

CELEBRATING
NOTRE DAME

PHOTOGRAPHY BY MATT CASHORE
TEXT BY KERRY TEMPLE
FOREWORD BY REV. JOHN I. JENKINS, C.S.C.

Published by Corby Books,
A Division of Corby Publishing
Box 93, Notre Dame, IN 46556

Book Design by Noah Armstrong

ISBN 0-9776458-2-7

*Printed In The United States of America
By Lithotone, Inc. of Elkhart, Indiana*

First Edition, August 2007

1 3 5 7 9 10 8 6 4 2

To my wife Maria, and my parents Tom and Adaline Cashore

— MC

My biggest thanks go to Kerry Temple. Simply put, this book would not exist without him. Thank you, Kerry, for all the adventures making pictures for *Notre Dame Magazine.* They have been learning experiences both as a photographer and as a person. The list of people who have helped me with this project and in my career is longer than the book itself but I'll try to name a few: Thank you, Joel Sartore, Matthew Landkammer, Ted Genoways, Mark Alstott, Amy Cashore, Anne Oulette, Don Nelson, David Amick, Tom Blicher, Marty Schalm, Nina Welding, Joanne Birdsell, Rev. Jim McDonald, C.S.C., Joe Raymond, Steve Peterka, Tim Prister, Joe Eufemi, Don Schoenfeld, Noah Armstrong, Tim Carroll and Jim Langford. Thanks to everyone at *Notre Dame Magazine,* and thanks to every Notre Dame staff member or police officer who ever unlocked a door, opened a roof hatch, put me up in a bucket truck or in some other way made one of my bizarre requests happen. I know I will remember dozens of others whom I should have mentioned by name, but know that your help was appreciated. And finally, thank you to my family.

This is for my parents, B.K. and Fayrine Temple

— KT

I would like to thank Matt Cashore whose stunning photography provided the inspiration for this endeavor and whose good-natured manner made the collaboration easy and right. I'd also like to thank Noah Armstrong for his skillful art direction, cooperation and expeditious labors as well as Jim Langford and Tim Carroll who saw merit in the project and took on the heavy-lifting of getting it done—with special gratitude to Jim for his editorial eye and for letting me use again a few paragraphs I had written specifically for *The Spirit of Notre Dame,* a book he and his son Jeremy had published in 2005.

I'd also like to thank all those who through the years have taught me what Notre Dame and the Notre Dame family are all about, especially Father Ted Hesburgh, C.S.C., Denny Moore, Dick Sullivan, Father Robert Griffin, C.S.C., John Houck, Ed Fischer, Jim Murphy, Jim Frick, Bill Sexton, Tom Werge, Joseph Brennan, Sister Jean Lenz, OSF, Dick Conklin, Andy Burd, Jim Gibbons, Father John Dunne, C.S.C., Jane Pitz, Chuck Lennon, Paul Wieber, Brother Joe McTaggart, C.S.C., Matt Storin, Larry Cunningham, Dan Reagan, Jim and Marilyn Bellis, Dan Saracino, Bob Schmuhl, Carl Magel, Jim Roemer, Dave Morrissey, Jim Malloy, Sam Hazo, Mike Garvey, Mamie Briscoe, Melanie Chapleau, Mike McDonough, Dave Wuellner, Dan Duffey, Chip Naus, Steve Reifenberg, Dick Duffey, Alex Montoya, Spike, Critter, Fitz, Mike Welch, Jim Wilson and the Farley Hall Molemen as well as my colleagues and good friends at *Notre Dame Magazine*—Walt Collins, Ron Parent, Carol Schaal, John Monczunski, Don Nelson, Julie Ettl, Ed Cohen, Mary Pat Dowling and John Nagy. And the others I've missed, forgotten, left out or whose names I never knew whose gifts and guidance are similarly appreciated as is my wife Jessica who has given me a whole new sense of the meaning and memory of Notre Dame and family.

FOREWORD

A PICTURE CAN DO MORE THAN FREEZE A MOMENT; it can capture people and places in a way that reveals both spirit and story. According to a maxim often attributed to St. Francis of Assisi, we should preach always, and use words when necessary.

Notre Dame does a lot of its communicating without words. There are many stories of people simply experiencing the campus and immediately building a bond of understanding and affection. No small part of our public visibility in recent years has been accomplished through the photographs of Matt Cashore, whose work is featured in this book.

Our multi-dimensional approach to people is possible partly because we are a place that has been blessed with great beauty—both the natural kind and the work of human hands. We know that beauty and truth go hand in hand, so we are happy to let scenes like the Golden Dome, our statues and buildings, the colors of autumn around our lakes, and the joyful fellowship of our students all speak for themselves.

The messages of these things which we see and hear are often so profound, so eloquent, that we fall silent. In some of life's richest moments, we stop reaching for words.

Sometimes, our appreciation of the sights of Notre Dame is silent. Sometimes, it's downright boisterous. Either way, it's a real communication with real messages, conveyed conscientiously and received attentively. Despite the lack of verbal input, and sometimes because of it, this communication has the power to bring us together, to bridge barriers of language and background, and to help us realize that we

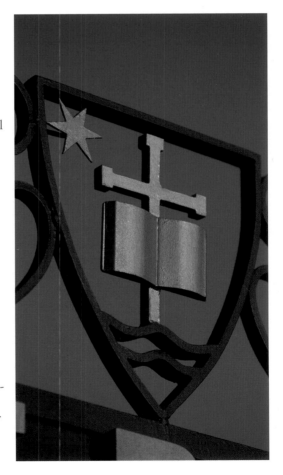

really are humbly united in an ongoing dialogue about great ideas, profound truths, and noble ideals. As St. Augustine puts it, "We see by the radiance of a light that is not our own."

That's why I am glad that the theme of this collection of images and reflections is "celebration." It's contrarian in our over-stimulated, often frenetic age to think that perusing through photos, letting these subtle slices of external reality touch our minds and hearts, could constitute a celebration. Where's the noise, the setting-loose of our instincts, the rush of adrenalin?

Indeed, it's contrarian in this "visual" age to think of making a big deal out of a photograph. Even though we seem to take hundreds of pictures with digital cameras and cell phones at the slightest instigation, our days are inundated with images that distract rather than inform us. We addictively speed from image to image with little thought or appreciation or real communication. Image is everything, and nothing.

Celebration, which means "to gather in order to honor," is a good word for the contrarian way in which Notre Dame approaches photographs or other images of life. These are scenes, settings, and sensations that reflect important meanings and priceless joys. Our radar picks up the presence of a memory and the possibilities of a moment.

As we celebrate the past and present of Notre Dame, we are also drawn to consider its future. The dream of Notre Dame was Fr. Sorin's one-hundred and sixty five years ago, and we are the heirs of that dream. Much of Sorin's dream has been realized, but so much more needs to be fulfilled and enlarged. There is more to be done. As we look toward the future, we strive to make Notre Dame an even more accomplished place of teaching, learning, and discovery. We want it to be ever more a powerful force for good in the world and

So we return to the theme and the contents of this book. This celebration of the image and likeness of the spirit of Notre Dame resonates with me—and with you, I'm sure—because it shows us what we have already come to know, and it draws us together through this recollection. The channels of communication are wide open in Matt Cashore's evocative photos of peace, intensity, and great potential, as they are in Kerry Temple's affectionate text touring the Notre Dame landscape and mindscape. The artistry in this book can surely pull you into some energizing times of conversation and contemplation. The artistry of our lives entails our going forth to paint, as it were, on an even bigger canvas.

For my part, I have been gratified to learn from many members of the Notre Dame family that they share the vision of Notre Dame to which I have committed my presidency. Our mission is to "go and tell … what we have seen and heard." (Luke 7:22) Our pictures are worth a thousand words, and our words are worth a thousand pictures. Our testimonies will vary, but we have photographic evidence that "all things work for good for those who love God." (Rom 8:28).

We have a lot of communicating still to do, in words and in pictures. With help from all members of our community, their many talents, and their enthusiasm to make Notre Dame's message their own, we can reach out to a sometimes fragmented and uncelebrating culture. We are grateful for, and strive to deepen and share with the world, the gifts we have received. We strive to live, individually and communally, in a way that inspires people, rekindles their hope, and invites them into celebration.

—Reverend John I. Jenkins, C.S.C., President
    University of Notre Dame

the Church. Where others see incompatible aspirations, we see creative tensions. We want to be a place that educates students to be influential and accomplished leaders in their chosen field, and to be humble and generous servants to those in need. We want to be a place where faculty are at the leading edge in inquiry and scholarship, and dedicated and effective teachers of our students. We want to be a diverse place, and to be a place of community and solidarity. We want to be a university in South Bend, Indiana, and to be a gathering place that is aware of and open to the world. We want to be counted among the best universities in the land, and to be a place of faith with a distinctive Catholic mission. We want to be a place of generous sacrifice, and a place of celebration.

INTRODUCTION

IT WAS LOVE AT FIRST SIGHT FOR NOTRE DAME AND ME.
I was just a boy, maybe 12, riding in the backseat of a car rolling up
Notre Dame Avenue. I kept trying to see the Dome, careening from
windshield to window, peering through the lush trees to spy the
Golden Dome looming large and tall against the blue Indiana sky.
My family had come a thousand miles to be here. I was missing school
to make the trip. "That's OK," Sister Eugenia had said, reassuring my
parents. "It's God's country. Once he sees it, he'll never be the same."
I had seen photos of the Dome. I had seen domes before—churches,
capitols, monuments on battlefields. But none of that had prepared
me for this. Wherever I went that day—by the lakes, the Grotto, the
Main Quad—the Dome was there. It stretched to the sky, towered
above campus, peered through giant maple, sycamore and oak. A
summit, a presence, a landmark, a symbol.

Years later, after I had seen the Alps and Rockies, and had been
moved by their lofty pinnacles and precipices, I wondered if this gilded
mountaintop rising above the Midwestern landscape—with its exuber-
ance of peaks, turrets, angles and protuberances—had not initially
seized my imagination for much the same reason. The Dome, too,
was rooted firmly in solid earth while seeming to rise right up to the
heavens. Of course, these thoughts did not come till much later. But
even that very first day, there was something about the Dome and its
crowning statue of Mary that touched my spirit, made my heart climb.
Even now, all these years later, that initial magic persists.

But it wasn't just the Dome. It was the lakes, the Grotto, the
Main Quad. It was the log chapel, perched on a hillside and tucked

O'Shaughnessy to the Rock, the front circle, the trees, the grass, I felt it. I sensed something more than what my eyes could see. Something in the air, something I walked through, something about the place that felt different, that felt right, felt true, felt like home, or something close to home, something I knew inside, that came not through my eyes but through the pores of my skin. Maybe something spiritual, holy, sacred. But whatever it was, I knew it right away. And I learned over time that I was not the only one to meet Notre Dame this way.

Many others have spoken of similar arrivals, have talked or written about their first time, their own meaningful introduction —football game, or impulsively pulling off the toll road, or landing here bags in hand ready to launch their college education, or the newest pilgrim delivered by a family member to this hallowed promised land. A first meeting, a friendly stranger, some rich, intoxicating first impression. All immediately moved by the grace of this place.

And I—even at age 12, I knew this is what college should feel like, found a home and destination, and boldly told my parents, "I will get the grades if you get the money," a declaration still recounted with smiles when family stories are told, a vow I made good on because of five years of single-minded diligence. Only then (after I had gained admission), did my parents—neither of whom had attended college—tell me that it had been their dream since the day I was born to have a son go to Notre Dame. The day I received my letter of acceptance, my father and I read it side by side in the kitchen. Then he pulled me into his arms and hugged me—for the first time I could remember (at least since I was very little).

This is what Notre Dame does to people.

For years now I have thought about this, about the power and allure of Notre Dame, about its mystique and presence. What is it really? Where does it come from?

Undeniably, it comes from people, the many, many good people who have inhabited this place, have given themselves to it, given themselves to others, those whose "blood is in the bricks," as

into brush, the creaky water pump, blocky Old College, the aged remnants of charming rusticity and simple beginnings. It was the campus architecture and yellowish bricks and the abundant beauty of trees. It was Tom Dooley's letter and the flickering candles nearby. The Huddle, the solemn serenity and stained-glass windows of Sacred Heart Church. The muted statues of Sorin, Christ and Corby. And the students—all male then and bundled against chilly autumn winds—bearing books and striding so purposefully, making their way briskly from building to building, as if important, demanding things were happening here.

But it was not as much what I saw as what I *felt*.

As soon as I first walked the quads, first passed between Sorin and Walsh halls, emerging onto the leafy Main Quad, or first stood there between Alumni Hall and the law school, looking long from

the venerable professor Frank O'Malley used to say. The litany is long and often personal, although some names show up time and again on many people's list. Hesburgh, Griffin, Lenz, Evans, Toohey, Werge, Dunne, Emil T. and countless others like these. The common thread is giving. Teaching, caring, touching lives, knowing the importance of people. The human touch. And knowing that Notre Dame means taking care of people, taking the time to care, and that there is something about the whole enterprise, the community, the legacy and traditions, that transcends the individual, the moment in time, that is bigger than any one person, and yet somehow calls upon each person to extend the reach, to spread the inheritance. Throughout its history Notre Dame has been enriched by this generosity of spirit, has befriended generations with a kindness of heart. The Notre Dame family is no myth.

Many attribute this presence, Notre Dame's grace and spirit to Our Lady atop the Dome, for whom the place is named and to whom the school is dedicated, whose guidance, hand and holy intervention have steered the institution through troubled, threatening times, and whose sense of love, dedication and sacrifice could be said to be the model of human endeavor here. Prayers laid before the Grotto are often astoundingly answered; Sorin's 19th century visionary promises and prophecies have come true. More than one University president has said the place owes to its matriarch all that has been accomplished here.

And what accomplishments there are: from log-cabin beginnings in the Indiana frontier to an internationally known institution of higher learning, overcoming great odds,

rising above its humble origins to become one of the nation's most visible, most celebrated universities, a symbol of Catholic achievement in a world that did not take kindly to Catholic aspirations. Notre Dame has indeed become an icon of Catholicism for an entire nation of Catholics who pointed to the institution with pride and admiration and who visit campus with the fervor of a religious pilgrimage. Immigrant Catholics establishing a foothold in this new world sent their sons here; it was *the* college—still is—for generations of the best and brightest Catholic scholars, young and old.

Early in the 20th century the school's football teams represented the triumph of underdog ambition and eventually symbolized the arrival of immigrant Catholics in the mainstream of American culture as well as others coming of age here, wanting to belong, to make it, to

succeed in a society once—perhaps still—skeptical of the marriage of Catholicism and scholarship, faith and reason, religious vigor and intellectual zeal. Even sport and study. Like many people, my initial awareness of Notre Dame came through football. And when a boyhood hero of mine signed a letter of intent to play baseball and basketball at Notre Dame, the announcement was front page news in Shreveport, Louisiana. I remember George Restovich's statement in the paper that day: "It's every Catholic boy's dream to go to Notre Dame." So I figured it must be my dream, too.

There did come a time, though, when I wasn't so sure. It was 1970, and I was a high school senior. I had been accepted to Notre Dame, and since I first stepped onto campus as that spellbound sixth grader, it had been the only place I had wanted to attend. Now I was having second thoughts. I was tired of working so hard and I knew I'd be in over my head at Notre Dame. I also knew Notre Dame was then seen as a kind of Catholic service academy. There were no girls, no social life, no cars, the only fun a pickup basketball game at the Rock and a room full of guys.

My sister Kenton was a senior at Saint Mary's College that year and my family was in South Bend from Louisiana for a visit. It was colder and greyer and windier than I imagined Siberia to be. I was thinking a warm-climate state university was the place for me as our family drove slowly between the Rockne Memorial and Saint Mary's

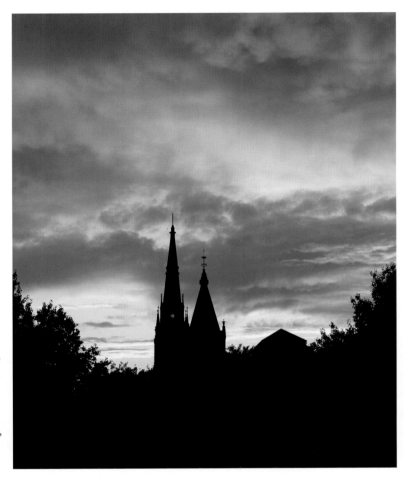

Lake. The lake was frozen solid, and I had never seen such a thing, and my sister was talking about all the ducks on the lake, and my mother asked, "But where do the ducks go in the wintertime?"

Few people would understand the poignancy of this question, but I—an avid reader of J.D. Salinger's *The Catcher in the Rye*—knew its significance, for during Holden Caulfield's flight to New York City he is concerned about the ducks in Central Park in winter. On several occasions he asks just that: "Where do the ducks go in the wintertime?" So my mother's question carried an eerie echo, and I looked to the lake and saw, dotting its frozen surface, whole flocks of ducks—looking miserable perhaps, but holding their own on the Siberian landscape.

Then, as the car turned past the Grotto, my sister said, "They stay here I guess," and just then I looked up and saw the Dome. It was shining brilliantly.

There are indeed moments in life when clarity blooms, when elements align in a moment that seems providential. That was one such moment, when the gleaming Dome appeared as a call to port, a beacon heralding the uncorrupted good that Holden longed for. Back then I did not know Notre Dame that well, but it stood for me as a place that was right and true, that had grounded itself in a certain common-sense goodness, that was on course trying to serve the world while not *being of* the world, by bringing together the proper blend of heart and soul, intellect and athletics. It was true to itself and true to those qualities and principles I wanted more of. I came here to learn.

And yet I soon learned that Notre Dame is so much more than even all this. It is classrooms and laboratories, residence halls and residence hall chapels. Fair Catch Corby, Touchdown Jesus and No. 1 Moses. The Hesburgh Library and Rolfs, Reckers and the Rad Lab, Kellogg and Kroc, lectures and late-night conversations. It's performances in Washington Hall and DPAC, exams in DeBartolo and Nieuwland, dinner at the dining hall, trips to the post office, the laundry, the Center for Social Concerns. Notre Dame is the ceremony and ritual of a football weekend and the celebration of Mass at Sacred Heart Basilica. It's long and lonely nights of isolation in a dorm room and the crowded jubilation of a rock concert or basketball game. It's roommates and classmates, professors, mentors and rectors, girlfriends, boyfriends, friends for life. It is memories and dreams, disappointments and life-changing experiences.

Notre Dame is largely the reflection of its founding order, the Congregation of Holy Cross, whose presence, leadership, and pastoral, spiritual and intellectual vitality have permeated the institution, its classrooms and most certainly its residence halls throughout the school's history. It is 160 years of folklore and tales—of mosquitoes and dams and Holy Cross brothers sent to find treasure in the California gold rush of 1849, of Father Lange, Al Sondej and King

Kersten, traveling statues and ghosts in Washington Hall—handed down from one generation to the next, senior to freshman, father to daughter. It's the stories lived here, and the ones swapped at reunions and tailgaters, UND Nights and freshman orientation. The brawl with the Ku Klux Klan, tug-o-war with an elephant, the time I stayed up all night and chowed down at Fat Shirley's before showing up for that final exam in economics. These are the stories that speak of Notre Dame, that convey the place, that carry on the tradition like family heirlooms passed to those who come after. They tell of a place that eludes, even defies the sharp focus of definition.

Those who have been touched by Notre Dame know how I felt when I first landed here. Many have come to live and tell their own stories. They have their own friends and favorite places, their own eras and points of emphasis—all-nighters in Bond Hall, a religious retreat or hall Mass, or crossing paths providentially with the guy who knew exactly what you were going through here, being different from the others, and who buoyed you through some dark night of the soul. But in many ways, what we all have had in common, what's been constant since 1842, is the very place itself. The lakes, the trees, the relatively flat Indiana landscape. The architecture of faith and learning. Buildings infused with memories. The edifices that harbor ghosts. Even though much has been added, the essential Notre Dame has been the same for decades, over a hundred years. The place is fully brimming with the phantoms of its past, the heritage of its rich history, the excitement of college life—a chapter in each Domer's life-book that is special and precious, intensely lived, irreplaceable, irrevocable.

But there is something more, something beyond all this, and it was as true that very first day as it is on this day, walking the campus, looking back and remembering. There is, within this place called Notre Dame, some ineffable presence, a spirit, a soul that permeates the physical, tangible reality of campus. A touch of the divine dwells here. And we feel it, I think, because that quiet, mysterious presence resonates with something deep inside us—some other ineffable presence, spirit or soul that responds to this sacred and very special place. I felt it when I first came here, and I have felt it through the years—the realization that here there is no barrier, no division between the physical world we know through our five senses and the spiritual reality we know in our heart. Notre Dame, in its very landscape and architecture and geography, is infused with and animated by this holy moment. And those open to its touch are blessed by its stunning emission of grace.

Richard Sullivan was an English professor who taught literature and writing for decades. I did not have him as a teacher, but visited him in his later years, when I was young and eager to learn all I could of Notre Dame. In a book of his, *Notre Dame: Reminiscences of an Era,* he wrote: "When you walked you were surrounded by the place, by an atmosphere, by a whole embracing, exciting, confirming tradition. Down a flight of stairs, around a bend, in the hall chapel, there was God." During one of our visits he told me, "Some things go beyond words. There are elusive yet obvious feelings, even facts, you cannot find words for. You can only suggest them. Poems can be written about Notre Dame, but not definitions."

I have now spent 32 of the past 36 years of my life at Notre Dame, as a student, teacher and employee, most of those years on the staff of *Notre Dame Magazine.* I have read volumes about the University, have talked about this rich, textured and complicated place with hundreds of people, have edited and written books about it, and have written countless articles, essays and stories about this

uniquely layered institution—about its Catholic character and academic ambitions, about the sense of community, residence hall life and coeducation, about pioneering research, the Congregation of Holy Cross, and the impact of great teaching on generations of students. Dick Sullivan was right. You *can* sense God's presence here. And you can tell stories *about* Notre Dame; you can speak *of* Notre Dame. But you cannot say for sure just what Notre Dame *is.*

For someone who has spent a lifetime using words to convey meanings, it is a curious admission to say that certain concepts, ideas and truths simply cannot be captured by language. All you can do sometimes is tell stories, create scenes or offer good words, and then hope that meanings might reveal themselves, might land within the head or heart of others. And sometimes you envy the photographer who seems able to capture in image the very scene that a writer must labor to describe. Notre Dame's is a picturesque, photogenic campus; it offers a good photographer any number of nice calendar shots, rich details, moving vistas and stunning panoramas.

Some photographers, though, are capable of presenting not only beautiful images but also the very *feel* of the place, the excitement and serenity, the earnest bustle of college life and the pastoral ease and holy solitude of the Notre Dame landscape—as well as the sense and meanings that elude the scope of definitions, that are beyond the province of words, until the images themselves are evocative of meanings and memories known to us all.

Matt Cashore is just such a photographer. Matt has been shooting Notre Dame since his students days in the early 1990s. Anyone who has paid any attention to *Notre Dame Magazine* over the past decade or who has seen almost any University publication or visited its Web site has seen his work. And seeing his work is to admire his ability to photograph campus life in a way that not only captures the beauty and poignancy of a stolen moment but also to convey that sense of Notre Dame that the eye cannot see, that is, rather, felt or sensed or somehow experienced by being present within the aura of the place. Matt might say it's about composition and viewpoint and catching the light just right, but his pictures catch the spirit, too. Like meaning that can be read "between the lines," Matt's photos bear meanings, memories, sensations and feelings present somehow within the two-dimensional images.

Matt has been photographing Notre Dame and variations on this theme for 20 years, yet his images are persistently fresh, the view through his lens perpetually innovative, his eye ready to see new meaning in familiar terrain, to catch the predictable moment from the unexpected angle. When I suggested *Notre Dame Magazine* present a sampling of his work in a photo essay in our summer 2005 issue and when our readers sought prints of their favorites, the time seemed right to bring them together in a book that spoke of Notre Dame.

Both of us observe the institution through our own eyes. But the intent of this book is to celebrate the common ground, to showcase a Notre Dame we all know, to let others see what we see but perhaps fashioning those windows to enable others to gaze out upon the landscape with a renewed appreciation or happy homecoming. In some ways, for each of us, this homecoming is a very personal one, and is most evocative of our students days. Despite all the interceding years I've spent at this University, the Notre Dame of memory and dream, the Notre Dame that is most vivid to me, is the Notre Dame I knew years ago as a student.

That Notre Dame was largely an all-male institution, composed mostly of sons from middle-class working families responsibly bearing their parents' hope of a better tomorrow. It was a vibrantly Catholic university but one still responding to the call of Vatican II, still adjusting to the societal rebellions and revolutions of the 1960s. It was a Notre Dame of pep rallies and football games, of tough coursework, lonesome times and the totally unique atmosphere of an all-male culture dominating residence hall life. It was a place of intimate debate and idealistic aspirations, the liberating exploration of belief and faith running headlong into scientific scrutiny, secularization and a world blown open by riots and war, demonstrations for peace and protests against Establishment custom and conformity. It was also about beer drinking and girl hunting and book reading and walking around the lakes, about pickup football on the quads, and the making of friendships that have lasted a lifetime.

What I loved most about my undergraduate days at Notre Dame was the dialogue, the conversation. I loved reading books and going to class, hearing lectures, getting exposed to divergent views, opinions, beliefs, listening to guest speakers and scholars, and taking those conversations back to dorm rooms, to the residence hall corridors, or to dinner, or to Louie's or Rocco's or Corby's where we'd drink beer, eat pizza, and talk about God and sports and the meaning of life and what we'd do to make the world better.

For me, Notre Dame was the confluence of freshman biology, Mark Twain and Willa Cather, Taoism, Shakespeare and the koans of Thomas Merton. It was Austin Carr, Ara Parseghian and Collegiate Seminar—that two-semester "great books" course in which 15 or 20 of us met in the Farley Hall lounge for three hours each Monday night to explore the week's readings. Two students would present papers, lead the discussion *and* contribute a couple of gallons of wine to make sure the conversations went well. We talked Plato and Freud, Black Elk and Confucius, Thomas Aquinas and Karl Marx. Here we were—dirtballs, hippies and pseudo-intellectuals—talking about war and peace

and God, corporate America, evolution and materialism, the role of government and how to get along … then going back upstairs to test our good intentions in the smelly, warty mix of all-male communal living.

For those four years I greedily partook of the ancient, hallowed liberal arts education, proceeding merrily along (much to my parents' dismay) heedless of any thought to future employment or vocational training. It was a great time of exciting, earnest dialogue, of student and faculty coming together enthusiastically exploring, expanding and resolving—a time and place perhaps best described by Dick Sullivan when he wrote: "The characteristic spirit of this University seems to me one of considerable intellectual tension. The people here strike me as exhibiting a remarkable concern—I should say a primary concern—for ideas, principles, values, theories, facts and the terrific illumination generated by the friction and occasional collision of all these.

"The very fury with which we quarrel confirms me. Clash of conviction is the honest noise made by intellects in action. And at Notre Dame there is perhaps an increased volume and a special clarity because here, clashing, we still speak a common language and share a common faith and intention. We have, as they say, a core."

But it was the second semester senior year when the meaning of Notre Dame was most poignantly distilled for me. Each afternoon, MWF, I went to Chris Anderson's abnormal psych class. There I learned the truth about human nature—stimulus-response and B.F. Skinner, the mechanistic body, behavioral conditioning, brain chemistry, and the neuroses of the religious. And I walked out of there thinking, yes, that is all there is, that is the human species, there is no soul, the rest is all delusion.

Then I walked over to Father John Dunne's theology class and listened to his lectures on the spiritual essence of life, the unseen and invisible, the mystical and the supernatural, and his moving examination of the path of the heart's desire. And as he paced back and forth, delivering truths like nuggets of flame, citing the guidance of Rilke, Kierkegaard and Kazantzakis, he would lift us and inspire, and paint whole new vistas of the wonders of infinite human nature.

For 30 years now that juxtaposition has stood for me as the most eloquent definition of my Notre Dame education—the sometimes uncomfortable meeting of the intellectual and the spiritual, the crossing of the worldly and eternal, the dazzling facets of truth that come from living the right questions. Notre Dame is a place where the ultimate and most elemental answers matter.

"Notre Dame," said Father Theodore Hesburgh, CSC, shortly after I graduated, "can and must be a crossroads where all the vital intellectual currents of our time meet in dialogue, where the great issues of the Church and the world today are plumbed to their depths, where every sincere inquirer is welcomed and listened to and respected by a serious consideration of what he has to say about his belief or unbelief, his certainty or uncertainty; where differences of culture and religion and conviction can co-exist with friendship, civility, hospitality, respect and love; a place where the endless conversation is harbored and not foreclosed."

It is hard to imagine a place more suited for this "endless conversation" than Notre Dame. Few institutions of higher learning in the world are as receptive to the full dimensions of that conversation as Notre Dame; none can bring forward the intellectual, moral, spiritual or material resources as capably as this catholic Catholic university. But the very campus itself encourages the Notre Dame experience as a time of study and learning, inquiry, contemplation and thoughtfulness. It is a still, deep pool in a world of rushing waters.

The campus offers a tranquil retreat from the world. It provides a refuge from the commotion of modern living, a place to stand back, step out, get away. For students *and* faculty, it is a place from which to study, analyze, behold, examine, observe, discuss. Even though what is here examined, observed, studied and contemplated is the world itself (and—importantly—ways the place and its people should be actively engaged in that world), the overriding environment here encourages a kind of time out, a pause, a platform from which to consider a variety of vantage points. It affords people a place to figure it out before taking rightful action.

While some have suggested the University's academic aspirations have been hurt by its distance from the great cultural centers and from its not readily interlacing with either an exciting urban environment or "college town" atmosphere, the setting provides its own merits. It is pastoral and park-like, putting those who live and work here in close touch to the natural world. The statues, architecture, chapels and religious iconography are quiet reminders of those eternal questions and concerns so easily lost in contemporary society. It is a

place of leisure and recreation, a runner's world, a place for walking, biking, roller-blading, even sitting—a place for solitude *and* the kind of surprising intimacy made possible by the quiet and peace of a sunset or a late-night walk or heartfelt conversation about the timeless issues that have faced humans for millennia. It is the kind of place where such conversations seem right and important and universally compelling. A place for education in the deepest, fullest sense of the word.

In the beginning Notre Dame was to be its own place. It had its own farm and farm animals, crops and kitchens, brick works, stables, tailors, cobblers, bakers, cooks, priests, teachers and students—a hummingly self-sufficient little enterprise carved into the Indiana wilderness. For decades that approach persisted and for decades after that a virtual moat was maintained to separate campus from the sins and vagaries of real-world city life surrounding it—and the resident priests made sure students would rarely and cautiously venture there. Today Notre Dame is still remarkably self-sufficient, taking care of its own utilities, running its own police and fire departments. For much of its history Notre Dame was intentionally monastic

in nature. That legacy is apparent today. Despite all the concessions to modern living and all the expansion outside its reticent borders, Notre Dame is still a place apart. And therein lies much of its charm, its appeal, its character.

I did not come back here to work in order to leave the world behind, to recreate my undergraduate days or because I was so attached to the place, or even to "give back" to the University for all it had given me. I came back because I wanted to be part of an endeavor outlined by Father Hesburgh in some documents in the late 1970s. I was working for a newspaper in Wyoming when Hesburgh described a Notre Dame with a calling to make the world a better place.

"Two predictions are fairly obvious," Hesburgh wrote 30 years ago. "First, there will be enormous changes that we can no more visualize or imagine than someone 50 years ago could visualize what was about to happen and at what a staggering rate of change; and second, one might predict that this changing world will confront humankind with enormous new moral problems of unprecedented proportion and consequences."

The priest then offered two further predictions: "Universities, the font of most human knowledge and knowledgeable people, will be at the heart of generating the people who, in turn, will generate the change. And secondly, it will take a very special kind of university to direct change in such a way that humans do not destroy themselves and their world." Notre Dame, Hesburgh concluded, aspired to be the kind of institution to "undertake the dual task of transmitting and expanding knowledge, but at the same time, the more difficult role of educating persons with that sense of moral responsibility and judgment required to manage change and to use knowledge for mankind's betterment and progress, instead of for its destruction."

I came back to Notre Dame to be part of that enterprise, to help fulfill that vision, to be part of a larger, more effective effort than I was capable of pursuing alone. Besides, I really liked the idea of participating in that "endless conversation" and lending my voice to the University dialogue. I have been fortunate to have worked at a magazine that has engaged that conversation for decades, has taken the campus discussions to readers throughout the world, and has extended the University's reach and reflected its principles, values and ideals. It is not far, really, from those rich and invigorating student days when I'd be so excited about new ideas, lofty ideals and the animated wrangling that comes when diverse-viewed people want to hammer things out.

"We do mean to be a great university," Father Hesburgh explained back then. "We are open to all the great questions of our times. We are confident enough, of ourselves and our students, to look at a wide variety of possible answers and to be assured that new light will be brought to bear upon these problems as we discuss them in a Christian context. We have no problem with other universities choosing to do their discussing in what might well be a more restrictive context, more secular, less religious, more purely or exclusively scientific and technological. So be it. But we need not be defensive in placing the same discussion in a different context, more universal (which is the meaning of catholic), more Christian, more moral, more spiritual, more open to the transcendental, to God, but no less intellectual. We do what we do freely, and in the conviction that the times, and especially the future, will need such an approach."

That is the Notre Dame I came to love as an undergraduate and the Notre Dame I have believed in throughout the decades working here. It's a vision underscored by Hesburgh's successors, the idea of a Catholic university — simply put — applying its resources, scholarship, research and graduates to make the world a better place, the melding of intellectual longings and the good weight of moral, ethical and spiritual wisdom. That is a promise and a pursuit worth giving a life to.

I have been here long enough now to have seen a lot of the place, to have been disappointed in its human frailties, to have moved far beyond the rosy patina of memory, romance and sentiment. But when I have become disillusioned or grumpy, when I have witnessed too much of the politics and personalities, I take a walk. And the

campus, the very place itself, welcomes me as it did so many years ago. I have only to walk the lakes or sit alone at the Grotto or rest on a bench and watch awhile in order for the place to show itself again, to reside in me, to work its spell again. And I know then that there is something here, something about the place, something within the landscape itself, that transcends the human, that sustains the promise and the legacy, that suggests the smile of God.

That is a good environment in which to work. I have been here now for decades, have seen the seasons and the years turn one into the next. I have crisscrossed the quads untold times, made countless trips into buildings old and new, have looped the lakes a thousand times — alone as a 19-year-old trying to see my footprint in the world and years later with children who grew up on these same trails. I've walked here on snowy winter nights and on sultry summer days. I've seen generations of students come and go; I've made new good friends and sadly bid goodbye to others. I have seen the place mature, gaining some good things and losing others. Through it all, as my life has circled around the seasons, this campus, its trees and lakes, the buildings and people who have all walked these paths together, this place — Notre Dame — has meant what it did to me that very first day — a place rooted firmly in solid earth while seeming to rise right up to the heavens.

—Kerry Temple '74, October 2006

"Where ya from?"

"What's your major?"

"What hall you live in?"

These are the well-worn questions that really say, "I want to get to know you." You hear them and ask them a hundred times over those first days of the school year. When the academic engines are revving. And the campus surges into motion. With 10,000 students arriving—in a single August weekend—from points all over the globe. Goofy, hand-painted signs direct traffic, cabs and newcomers to almost thirty residence halls. Second-hand couches and dressers get pulled out of storage. Lofts get built, freshmen get oriented, cars unloaded. Parents stand by, watch, carry boxes, lift, hug, bid farewell—with pride and tears welling simultaneously. Their sons and daughters are on the ledge of tomorrow, hardly looking back. There are class schedules to sort out, books to buy, people to meet, a new slate of courses, professors, meetings and activities. New football season, too, with all those attendant hopes. Fresh start. New year.

Notre Dame is all about beginnings. It is where young people—idealistic, earnest, talented, intent—come to launch their dreams, their careers, their entrance into the wider world. From here they embark upon their explorations into various fields of study, professional opportunities, global issues, the complicated give-and-take of human relationships. Faculty, with an infectious passion for research and scholarship, become the mentors, scouts and visionaries, the role models for the academic enterprise and its sense of exploration, examination, experimentation. Each class, each book, each day is new … and each holds promise for what tomorrow might bring. The excitement is nearly palpable, the energy obvious and abundant. The contrast between summer and autumn is clear and extreme.

As much as anything else, fall at Notre Dame means football, and not just football games but the reunion, ritual and ceremony that is a football weekend on the Notre Dame campus. The marching band, the Irish Guard, the pep rallies and trips to a madly congested bookstore. The Shirt. The Leprechaun. The hot dog stands and brats and K of C steak sandwiches. The "step off" on the Main Quad. Tailgating. Bedsheet banners hanging from dorm windows. Good, old friends you see but once a year. Meet for pizza at Rocco's, a beer at the 'Backer, the concert on the steps of Bond Hall. Yes, and a football game, too. A half-dozen weekends a year the place is transformed from a college campus into a kind of Mecca for football-minded pilgrims — Fighting Irish fans as well as the followers of opposing teams who've heard there's no place like Notre Dame on a football weekend. A tradition to savor and uphold. A confirmation that this place is special.

"**H**ow ya doin'?" "How was your summer?" "What'd you do over break?" "How are things?" These are the welcome-back questions, the ones that say, "I'm glad you're here. It's good to be together again." These are the days, the times, the moments that make the Notre Dame experience a once-in-a-lifetime celebration, that remind old friends that you knew them when—back in the day your life was really starting, back when your dreams and aspirations were real and just beginning. A time and a place when it's all before you … and new … and resplendently unfettered.

Notre Dame is a keenly nocturnal creature.
So much happens after the sun goes down. Students seem to move under cover of dark. Treks to the library or LaFortune. Heading to movies and lectures. The Keenan Revue, Sophomore Literary Festival, SYRs, something doing at DPAC or Washington Hall. Trips to the neighborhood bars, off-campus harbors. Food sales. The hectic humming in *The Observer* offices, middle-of-the-night daily newspaper production. Bone-chilling tromps on snowy nights to basketball games at the JACC. Late-night studying, hanging out, video games till all hours, communal TV watching, reading, meeting, hooking up. Rolfs and the Rock pulsing, dancing with the combustion of youthful hyperactivity.

STUDENTS WHO GO THROUGH THE MOTIONS THROUGHOUT THE DAY COME ALIVE AT NIGHT, but not really till 10 or so, when the rest of the world is turning off, tuning out, turning in. The college-age cohort is on a different clock, different time zone. Midnight is early, hours to go before they sleep. Each day a feast, a circus, a caravan packed to overflowing—so much to fit in ... papers to finish, phone calls to make, exams to study for, good friends to laugh with.

BUT FOR THOSE SHUFFLING FROM ONE BUILDING TO ANOTHER—
after hours, late at night—silence envelopes the darkened campus.
Streetlamps illumine the inky corners; light pools on crisscrossing side-
walks. Muted voices are borne on nighttime breezes. The lattice-work
windows of residence halls glow reddish, gold and amber. Look inside.
The dorm-room walls are covered in posters, purloined signs and books.

   The sounds of music and laughter emanate from the cozy
confines where roommates study, tease and taunt, sometimes console
in hushed tones. Real living takes place here, where bunks and lofts,
rectors and friends and desks and all manner of electronic devices
crowd into these flourishing cells of human habitation. Indeed, this
just might be the very place where the real education takes place,
where the ideas, dreams and theories get plumbed and tested to see if
they mesh or clash with the inescapable, in-your-face reality of daily
life in earnest. Where everything is personal. Where you can never
really get away.

THE GROTTO IS THERE FOR THE PAUSING AND PRAYING.
Candles tremble and persist in the wind and the rain. The moon-faced
clock in the Sacred Heart steeple keeps watch. The Dome is a yellow
lighthouse; birds and bats play in its aerial glow. On starry nights and
under cover of cloud the campus teems with activity. And yet, it's the
solitude and serenity that comes through when you make your way
across the quads, buildings lit up on the inside, few people passing,
the wind on your face, your hair, like the breath of gods both gentle
and fierce, letting you know the spirits are close if you're still enough
to notice.

Notre Dame at night. There's a whisper at the ear, calling.

NOTRE DAME WINTERS SEEM TO DEFY THE LAWS OF PHYSICS.
In whatever direction you head across campus, you walk against
the wind. The Arctic gales scream down from Canada, travel the
length of Lake Michigan, and arrive unimpeded and undeterred in
Michiana—only to be funneled into a maze of wind tunnels slicing
the campus into whirring eddies that scour your face at every turn.
On Notre Dame's campus there is no tailwind; the wind is always
against you.

Winter at Notre Dame can hurt. It can be a grim, siege-like
assault on the senses, the psyche, the spirit, the soul. A pearl-white
permacloud can settle over the landscape for days, and the days
drudge by. Everyone stays indoors. "Cabin fever" sheds its mythi-
cal meaning and takes on a fearsomeness all too real. "Stir crazy"
too—and the concomitant hijinks and pranks, roommate squabbles,
snowball fights and dare-you streaking.

It is unimaginable to write of Notre Dame and not speak of weather—of the depressing and bone-chilling winters, the dreary rains of autumn and early-spring, the "unseasonable" cold, or the sultry days of September when no air moves through residence hall steambaths.

But I do love winter when the sky is blue and the air is crisp and tight as crystal, with snow blanketing the quads and rooftops, dolloped like whipped cream onto tree-trunks, limbs and bushes. It can be unearthly quiet—footsteps, voices and tires muffled by the acoustics of ice and snow. Sometimes, when the air is still and clean, I will stop and savor the elegance of this wintry wonderland, the purity and peace. The Dome is never brighter than on a glistening January day; the Grotto never more explicitly fervent than on a winter's night. I love walking campus in the dark of winter—quieter still than any daytime, and somehow radiant in the shadows made of snow, when everything is made visible against the white of winter's countenance. Even the buildings seem more inviting, as they offer warmth and refuge from frosted nights afoot. The cascading snow in all its faces and forms is beauty in flowing motion.

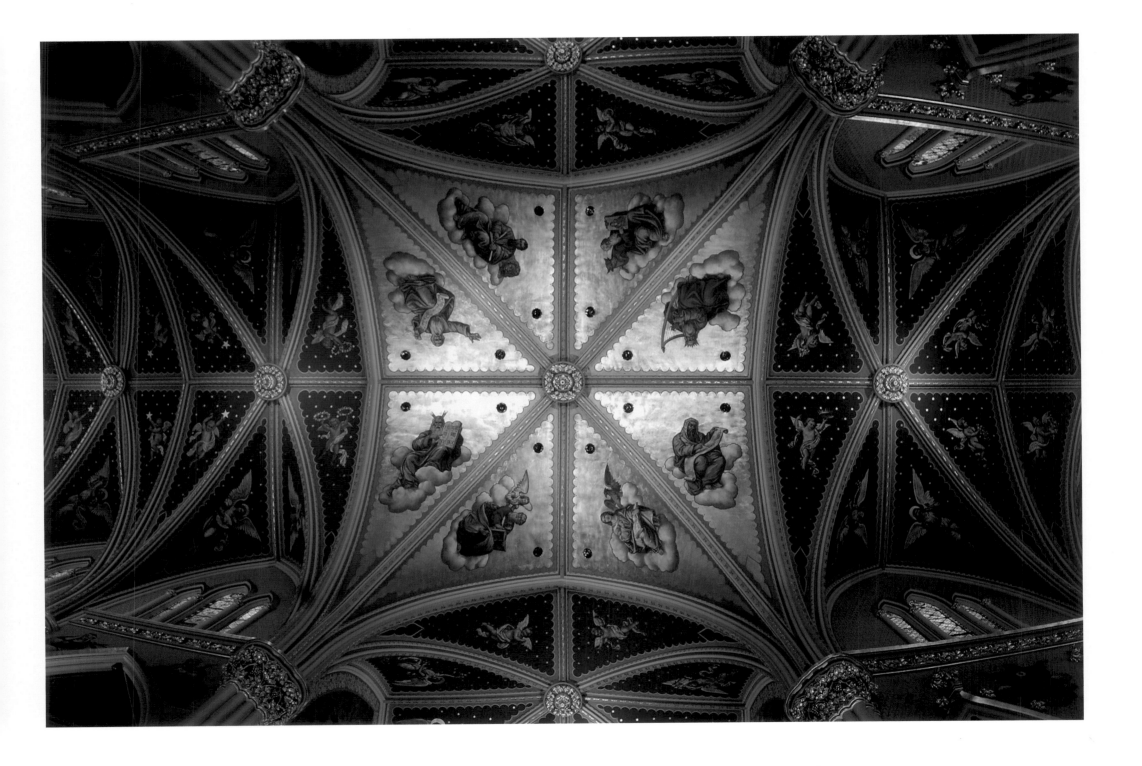

So few people walk the nights. That makes it better for those of us out and about, bundled against the cold that invariably evaporates when the exertion of body and serenity of place find their equilibrium. Too few people take in winter as they should. Those who grouse most are those most immune to winter's delights—even if one of those delights is hibernation … settling in with books and friends … nestling near the communal hearth … wrapping oneself in the cloak of studious contemplation, self-examination, the retreat and leap of prayer. Call it old-fashion and perhaps old-school Catholic, but I've often thought a Notre Dame winter forges a toughness and strength, a willingness and endurance that helps discipline the mind, that brings the proper pause to a young soul eager for epiphanies. The Notre Dame winter, surely the target of most Domer complaints about life in South Bend, is a considerable ingredient in the powerful concoction that is a Notre Dame education. It shapes and layers so much of what happens here. It is central to the identity of this place.

Despite winter's stoic face, one of my happiest, most palpable memories of winter here is the night a bunch of hallmates took this Louisiana boy to Saint Mary's Lake and strapped some ice skates on his feet and steered him onto that fast, glassy plane of ice. Initially stumbling and bumbling, I was coaxed into competence—and eventually I sailed. Never before had I felt so swift and so free, gliding so triumphantly from one end of the lake to the other. There was a bowl of brightly twinkling stars overhead, a thick drift of snow on the lake and land, cold air on my face, and holy golden light from the Grotto, the Dome, the windows of Morrissey, Lyons and old Holy Cross Hall—bright haloes of light shining through the wreathe of spidery trees whose bare and bony fingers embraced the place before me. Winter is Notre Dame's stark reminder of the earth's severe and elemental powers; it is a rugged path to life's grace, wonder and mystery.

I WALK THE LAKES WHEN I WANT TO GET IN TOUCH AGAIN WITH WHAT I FIND THERE.
It may not be that different from what Father Sorin found there one November day in
1842—or Father Stephen Badin, for that matter, that itinerant missionary who lived awhile in
a cabin on the hill just above the lakes (land and cabin later bequeathed to Sorin to start his
school). Even today you can get a sense of the native geography, especially there among the tall
trees to the west of the water. I think you can also get a sense of the deeper currents and life
forms that abound here, the spirit and sense of the place that predate the construction of so
many buildings.

Some choose—and rightly so—to find their solitary home at the Grotto, Sacred Heart,
or one of the tranquil hall chapels. We all need a quiet spot to reconnect, retreat, reflect, and
campus offers a nice selection. The lakes have always worked for me. I like to be outdoors; I
prefer walking to sitting (it exercises the mind as well and helps it cover good ground, too).
The paths around the lakes are surely part of campus, and yet not. They provide a bit of an
escape, a temporary respite and removal from all that happens in the classrooms, labs, dorm
rooms and offices where human trafficking can reach rush-hour proportions and pressure.

Notre Dame's is a walker's campus, and the trails that rim the lakes offer the best routes for walkers, joggers, runners. I have circled the lakes so many times through the years that I have nearly memorized the details in the terrain—the subtle rise and fall of the earth, the bends and curves, the troughs left by erosion, familiar tree limbs and roots, those spots favored by ducks, readers and lovers. I have favorite niches, too, and places I stop to look across the water at the buildings and rooftops, turrets and steeples across the way—the campus skyline. I have walked circles around the lakes when I have felt lost—as an earnestly searching student, and as a young man still trying to figure it out, and now in my middle years plagued by the same abiding questions and answers. I have run the lakes and ridden bikes around them. I have raised children on their banks, feeding the ducks and geese, catching fish, swimming at the beach there by the old boathouse, hanging out, exploring, just messing around, allowing for playful, imaginative leisure in a landscape made for that.

In the midst of whatever else is going on in my life I have always returned to the lakes. When I go there, it is like going home, to a place where you can settle in, take a seat, take a walk, take a deep breath, stretch out on the grass and stare at the sky … and be. Just being there brings a comfort and a peace, a rightness, a sense of intimacy with something you can't really see or taste or feel, except inside of you. Of course, it is partly about the water and the trees and grass, the moonlight shimmering upon the lapping waves, sunset look-ing west across Saint Mary's Lake, the time you swam the length of St. Joe Lake. The memories and the years. The dark nights of the soul and the romantic interludes. The gentle willows and giant sycamores.

But I also think it's the same thing Badin and Sorin found when they landed here, the thing that made them stop and say, "This is the place." You can sense it most anywhere on campus, but nowhere more purely than down there by the lakes.

THE VERY ARCHITECTURE IS UNMISTAKABLY TRADITIONAL.
"Collegiate Gothic" it's called, and even the most modern constructions are fashioned in this classic style. The religious statuary and yellowish bricks of the oldest buildings (made from marl dredged from the campus lakes) contribute distinctive Notre Dame accents and sensibilities. The buildings themselves say "tradition" and "Catholic," and pay homage to a rich and revered past. As well they should; Notre Dame basks in tradition.

The Main Quad, with its eclectic garden of trees and its statues of Christ and Sorin, is the campus heart and core. Those who know some history see evidence there of the cherished and age-old legacies. Sacred Heart, Sorin and Walsh stand as tangible monuments to the importance of religion and residentiality. Washington Hall, for more than a century, has provided the stage for artistic performances, lectures and readings. The Main Building, put up in about four months after fire wiped out its predecessor, once housed students, dining hall, offices, library and classrooms—a testament to Notre Dame's remarkable ingenuity, tenacity and sense of community. And the LaFortune Student Center and Hurley Building confirm that academics have had a central place on campus for decades. LaFortune was the Science Hall at turn of the 20th century, and pioneering research in flight and wireless communication took place there.

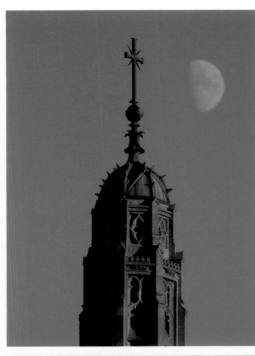

Notre Dame's efforts in scholarly research have certainly flourished in recent decades. The University has become much more serious about graduate studies and its graduate students have become more integral to campus life. The place is much more determined across all disciplines to be engaged in cutting-edge pursuits to create knowledge, generate technology and advance the frontiers of human culture and cultivation. The Jordan Hall of Science is the latest indication of Notre Dame's accelerating ambitions in the academic enterprise, but just off the Main Quad is the old chemistry hall where the formula for synthetic rubber was developed and Nieuwland where experiments into the structure of the atom have taken place for five decades.

When merged with the extraordinary quality of Notre Dame's undergraduate experience and the school's emphasis on exceptional teaching as the hallmark of a Notre Dame education, the scholarly enterprise is clearly robust—a tradition as esteemed and vital as any. The place clearly belongs in the front-rank of America's colleges and universities. It is a university in the fullest sense of the word … first and foremost an educational institution.

But Notre Dame is quite different from other schools with similar academic aspirations. It is undeniably Catholic, and its Catholicism permeates the place. The manifestations of faith are obvious: crosses and statues, the Grotto, the Mestrovic sculptures outside O'Shaughnessy, the Dome, the giant mosaic of Christ on the Hesburgh Library. Each residence hall has its own chapel and the weekly Masses infuse each with a sacred intimacy and community. Questions of faith, morality, ethics and spirituality are topics for classroom debate as well as informal dialogue—in hallways, over lunch, late at night, on the pages of *The Observer*. Theology and philosophy are required academic offerings. Campus Ministry, the Center for Social Concerns and other centers uniquely foster faith lives. The student body is decidedly Catholic; they are impressively involved in volunteer efforts. Much scholarship is mindful of issues of right and wrong, doing the right thing, cultivating Catholic social teaching and a Christian conscience. Despite the occasional calls to be vigilant in nurturing this crucial ingredient in the Notre Dame ethos, the University's Catholicism is healthy, vibrant and diversely textured.

Yet there is little doubt that the University's academic ambitions can pose rival demands to its fundamental Catholic traditions. The result is a creative tension that has animated the campus conversation for decades, if not from the very beginning. How does one give free rein to the intellect, the scientific method, to free will and reason, to the very ideals of the secular academy while following the tenets of faith and religious teachings that go back 2,000 years? That's an essential question whose complex and ever-evolving answers articulate Notre Dame's very nature.

It is not the only area where competing goals, values and principles rub against each other. How does the institution, for example, maintain its sense of community and humanity as it experiences astounding growth? How does it care for students entrusted to its guidance and supervision while fostering their maturity, independence and intellectual investigations? How does it boldly enter the future while embracing, even clinging to the foundations that have girded its past?

The truth is, even this apparent conflict between future and past is a Notre Dame tradition. Its founder was a 28-year-old visionary with a bit of the rebel, the renegade, the gambler in him. He was a French, Catholic priest in the New World, dreaming of a university in a still-wild frontier. And since its inception Notre Dame has been a place for such dreamers, for the forward-looking, for deans and scholars, researchers and presidents envisioning the future—and for students getting set for tomorrow. But it has also always been a place that remembered its past, its roots, its history and foundation, and has carefully tended those traditions so essential to its character.

THERE WAS A TIME when the running gag among students was that the best view of the Dome was in the rearview mirror. It was usually delivered to freshman by grinning upperclassmen to show they had outgrown the giddy Domer-style frolic of college life and were too mature for Notre Dame, with its juvenile restrictions, regulations and *in loco parentis* attitudes. So long, rules and regimentation, South Bend winters and lives wrapped in familial and communal obligations. But leaving is hard. I doubt any of those jaded seniors did not ache a little when they looked back over their shoulders at the Dome one more time. So much gets left behind.

Even those who count four years as enough and are now eager for life's next phase—the real world outside Camelot—the parting is difficult. And sad. And comes with a sense of longing and loss. For in the midst of accomplishment and liberation come stunning farewells and final hugs. There are last trips to the Grotto and final walks around the lakes. One more round at Corby's. One last time staying up all night talking.

I remember well just such a night—senior week, going out drinking, one long last farewell tour, one final trip to Fat Shirley's, the long walk back to campus, coming around Saint Mary's Lake near the Grotto on my way to Lyons Hall … then stopping with a few friends at sunrise, looking at some ducks along the water's edge, followed by a parade of fuzzy little ducklings—a new generation of ducks, I thought then, for the next generation of students. Then, too, I recalled an experience I'd had as a freshman grilling hot dogs on a football Saturday when a flock of alumni stopped by. They were rah-rah clad and laughing, talking, full of themselves and the moment. Even then I knew the place was no longer theirs; they could only pretend. They were expatriates—graduated, gone, forever now to be outsiders, interlopers, left with a past they could never quite relive, recreate or recapture.

Notre Dame belongs to its students. Even those who live and work here for decades know it is not really their place. It exists for the students, and it is theirs for a fleeting glimpse of years—a once-in-a-lifetime parcel of startling experiences, rich and vivid memories, life-changing journeys, and the powerful assault on the mind, heart and spirit that is college life du Lac.

I once told a high school senior who was trying to decide whether or not to enroll here, "You can go to college anywhere and get a good education, but Notre Dame will change your life." I once told a senior, who had said he wasn't going to commencement, to think again about what it meant. The ceremony is not just for the graduates and their symbolic launching into the world. It's a family celebration—meant to honor each family's achievement and the reality of dreams first imagined when parents read bedtime stories, taught the ABCs, and devoted their lives to a child's well-being. Graduation marks a passage in the whole family's life, and here at Notre Dame it is a very special keepsake.

THE NOTRE DAME NARRATIVE IS ONE OF GENERATIONS coming and going, the repeating cycle of lives passing into and out of this place, lives that compose and change the Notre Dame family, and lives forever altered by this rare and compelling institution.

When I drove away from Notre Dame as a graduating senior, I knew I had just finished the best four years of my life. That has not turned out to be true, but there has never been a time in my life so carefree and so fun, a time so full of such genuine camaraderie and intimate friendship, of such exciting personal explorations, the robust feeding of intellectual cravings, the wide-open pursuit of dreams, meaning and idealism, the sweet sense of life on the doorstep, horizons all clear and promising, beckoning.

Those feelings have stayed with me since, and being on campus rekindles those memories, dreams and emotions. It keeps those hopes and ideals alive. Notre Dame may belong to its students, but its graduates will belong to Notre Dame for the rest of their lives.

INDEX OF PHOTOGRAPHS
BY PAGE NUMBER